CHART HITS
OF 2018–2019

ISBN 978-1-5400-4720-5

HAL•LEONARD®

Visit Hal Leonard Online at
www.halleonard.com

Contact us:
Hal Leonard
7777 West Bluemound Road
Milwaukee, WI 53213
Email: info@halleonard.com

In Europe, contact:
Hal Leonard Europe Limited
42 Wigmore Street
Marylebone, London, W1U 2RN
Email: info@halleonardeurope.com

In Australia, contact:
Hal Leonard Australia Pty. Ltd.
4 Lentara Court
Cheltenham, Victoria, 3192 Australia
Email: info@halleonard.com.au

CONTENTS

Better Now

Words and Music by Austin Post, Carl Rosen, Adam Feeney, Louis Bell, William Walsh and Kaan Gunesberk

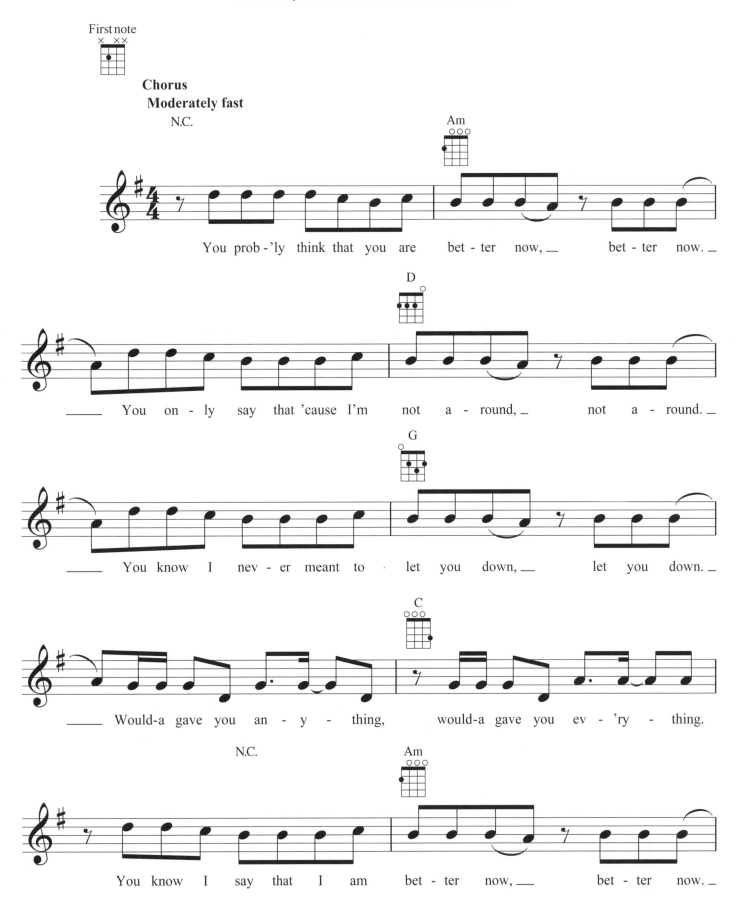

You know all my un-cles and my aunts, though. _____ Twen-ty can-dles, blow 'em out and

o - pen your eyes. _ We were look-ing for-ward to the rest of our lives.

Used to keep my pic-ture post-ed by your bed - side. _ Now it's in your dress-er with the

socks you don't like. And I'm roll - in', roll - in', roll - in', roll - in' _____ with my

broth - ers like it's Jo - nas, Jo - nas. _____ Drink - in'

Hen - ny and I'm try - na for - get, _____ but I

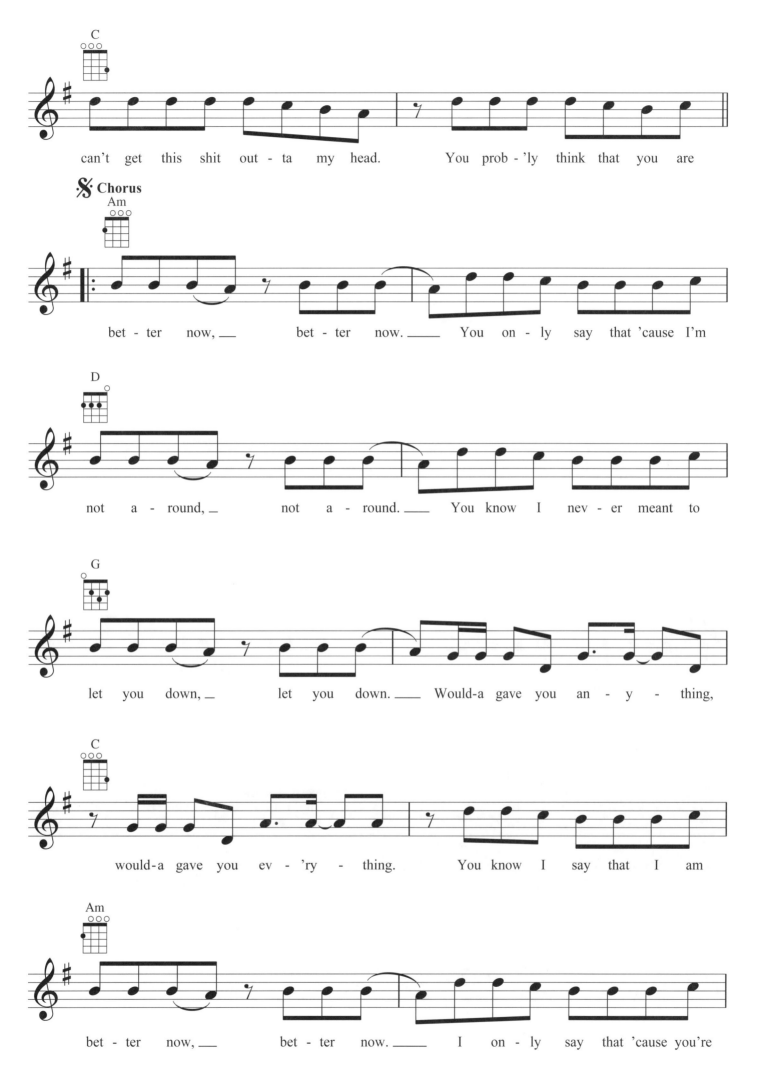

can't get this shit out - ta my head.   You prob - 'ly think that you are

Chorus

bet - ter now, __   bet - ter now. ___   You on - ly say that 'cause I'm

not a - round, __   not a - round. ___   You know I nev - er meant to

let you down, __   let you down. ___   Would-a gave you an - y - thing,

would-a gave you ev - 'ry - thing.   You know I say that I am

bet - ter now, __   bet - ter now. ___   I on - ly say that 'cause you're

not a - round, __ not a - round. ___ You know I nev - er meant to

let you down, __ let you down. ___ Would-a gave you an - y - thing,

would-a gave you ev - 'ry - thing, oh. _____

Verse

2. I seen you with your oth - er dude. He seemed like he was pret - ty

cool. _____ I was so bro - ken o - ver you.

Life, it goes on; what can you do? _____ I just won - der what it's gon - na take;

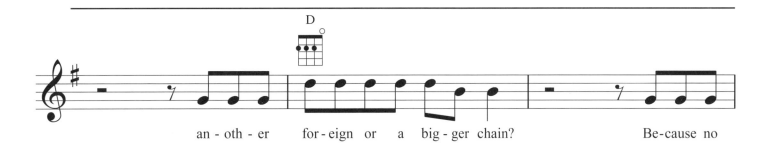

an - oth - er   for - eign or   a   big - ger chain?   Be - cause no

mat - ter how my life has changed,   I   keep on   look-ing back on bet - ter days.

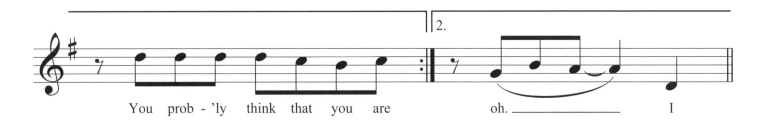

You prob - 'ly think that you are   oh. _____   I

Bridge

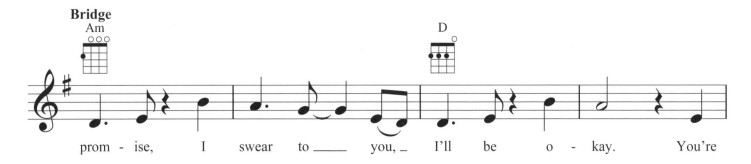

prom - ise,   I   swear to ____ you, _ I'll be   o - kay.   You're

on - ly   the   love   of ___ my   life. ___

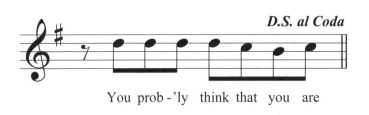

D.S. al Coda

You prob - 'ly think that you are

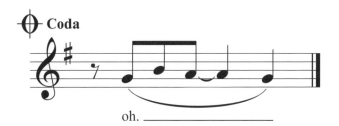

Coda

oh. _____

Breathin

Words and Music by Ariana Grande, Savan Kotecha, Max Martin and Ilya

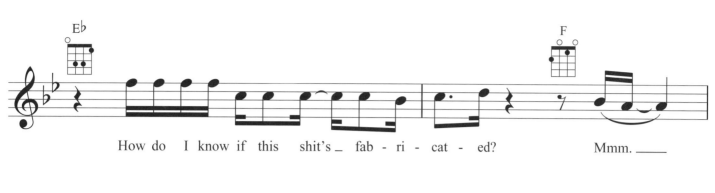

How do I know if this shit's _ fab - ri - cat - ed? Mmm. ____

Time goes by and I _____ can't con - trol my mind.

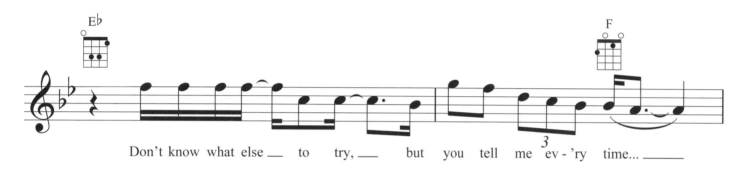

Don't know what else __ to try, ___ but you tell me ev - 'ry time... _____

Chorus

Just keep breath - ing and breath - ing and breath - ing and breath - ing. I know _

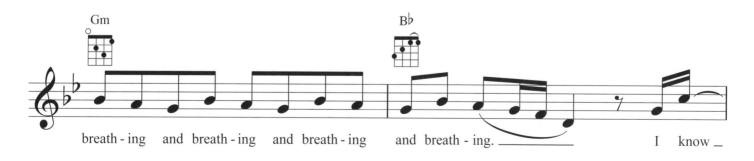

____ I've got to keep, keep __ on breath - ing. Just keep

breath - ing and breath - ing and breath - ing and breath - ing. _____ I know _

Broken

Words and Music by Mitchell Collins, Christian Medice and Samantha DeRosa

Interlude

_____ could be lone - ly with you. _____ (Instrumental)

2. There's some - thing trag -   Well, life is not a

Bridge

love song   that we   like.   We're all bro - ken   piec - es   float - ing

by.   Life is not a   love   song,   we can   try   to   fix our bro - ken

piec - es   one   at a   time.   I like _____

Chorus

that you're bro - ken, bro - ken like me. May -

- be that makes me a _____ fool. _____ I like _____

that you're lone - ly, lone - ly like me. I _____

could be lone - ly with you. _____ I like _____

1.

2.

Outro

(Instrumental)

1.

2.

Eastside

Words and Music by Benjamin Levin, Nathan Perez, Ashley Frangipane, Ed Sheeran and Khalid Robinson

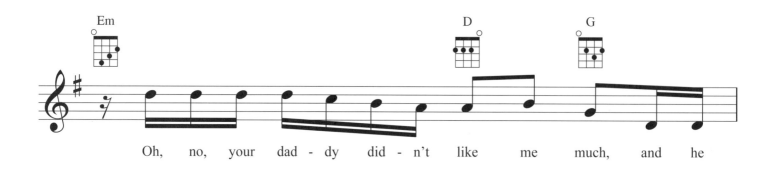

did - n't be - lieve me when I said you were the one.

Oh, ev - 'ry day, she found a way out of the

win - dow to sneak __ out late. She used to meet me on the

𝄋 Chorus

East - side, __ in the cit - y where the sun don't set. And ev - 'ry day, you know that

we'd ride through the back streets in a blue Cor - vette. __ Ba - by, you know I just wan - na

leave _____ to - night. __ We can go an - y - where __ we want, __ drive down __ to the

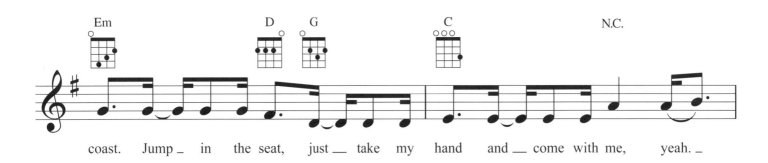

coast. Jump _ in the seat, just _ take my hand and _ come with me, yeah. _

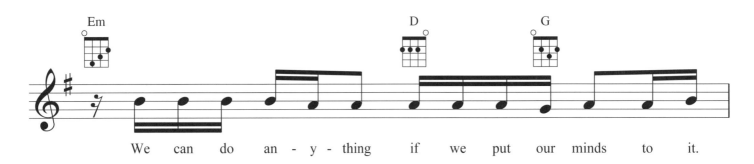

We can do an - y - thing if we put our minds to it.

Take your old life, then you put a line through it.

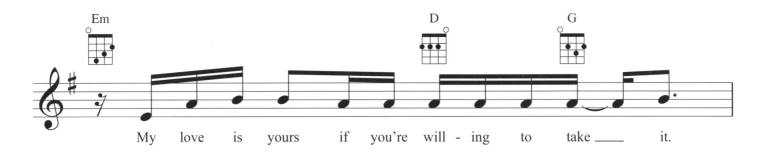

My love is yours if you're will - ing to take ____ it.

Give me your heart 'cause I ain't gon - na break ___ it.

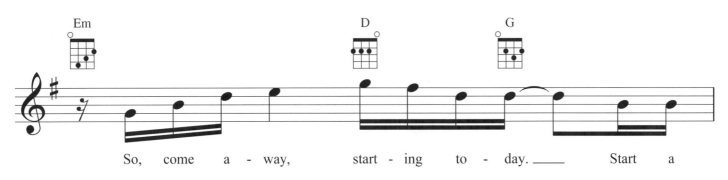

So, come a - way, start - ing to - day. ____ Start a

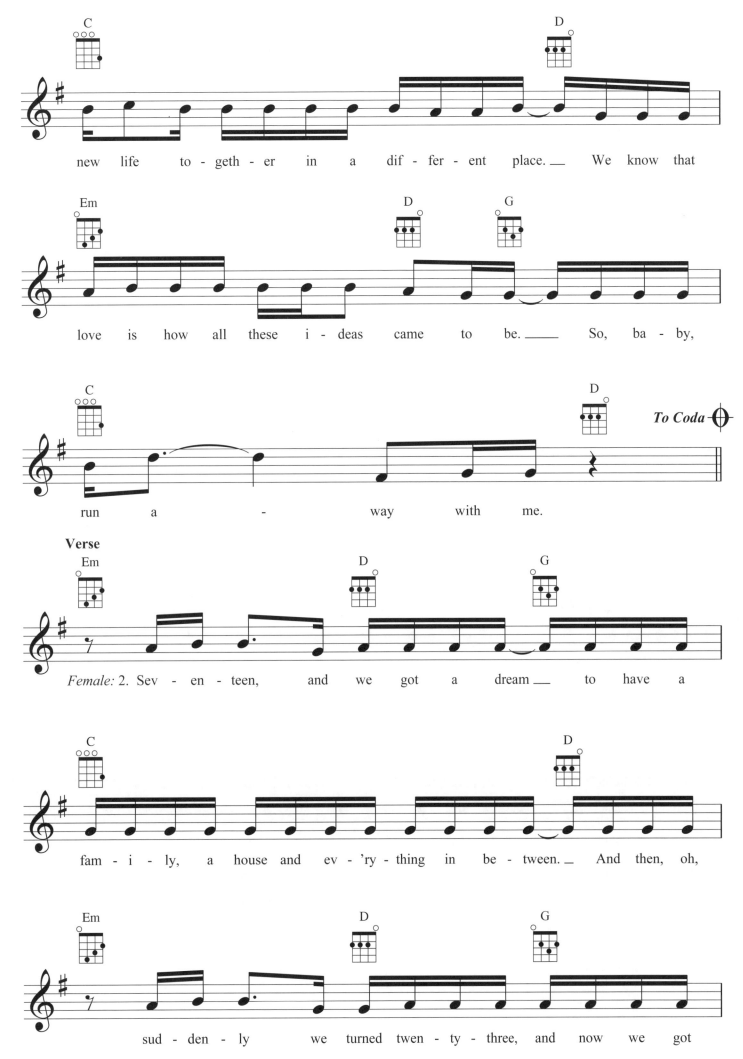

pres - sure for tak - ing our life more se - ri - ous - ly. _____ We got our

dead - end jobs _____ and got _____ bills to pay. _____

Our old friends _ are now our en - e - mies. And now I,

I'm think - ing back, to when I was young, _ back to the

D.S. al Coda

day when I was fall - ing in love. _ He used to meet me on the

Coda
Bridge

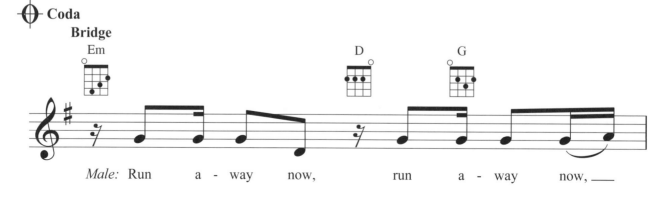

Male: Run a - way now, run a - way now, _____

run a - way now. Run a - way now, __ run a - way now,

run a - way now. *Female:* He used to meet me on the

Outro

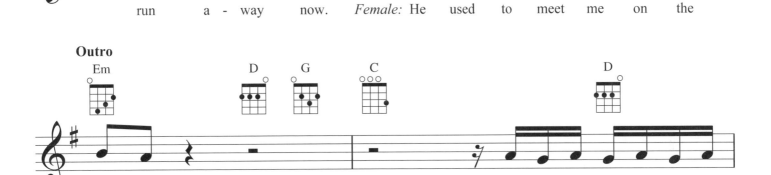

East - side. *Male:* She used to meet me on the

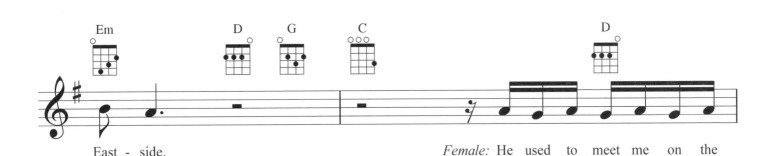

East - side. *Female:* He used to meet me on the

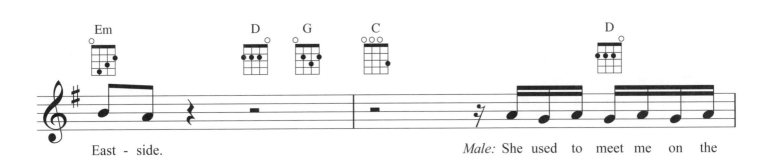

East - side. *Male:* She used to meet me on the

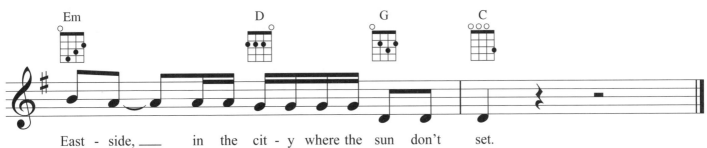

East - side, __ in the cit - y where the sun don't set.

Happier

Words and Music by Marshmello, Steve Mac and Dan Smith

think that we both know the way that the sto - ry ____ ends. Then,
least we can swim far a - way from the wreck we ____ made.

Pre-Chorus

on - ly for a min - ute, I want to change my mind 'cause this just don't feel

right to me. I want to raise your spir - its, I want to see you

smile, but know that means I'll have to leave. *(Instrumental)*

Know that means I'll have to leave.

Chorus

Late - ly, I've been, I've been think - ing I want you to be

like this,   I think that you'll be   hap - pi - er,   I   want you to be

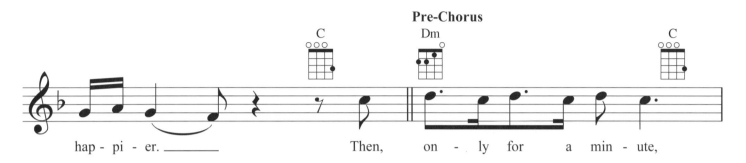

Pre-Chorus

hap - pi - er. _____   Then,   on - ly   for   a   min - ute,

I want to change my   mind 'cause   this just don't feel right   to   me.   I

want to raise your spir - its,   I want to see you smile, but   know that means I'll

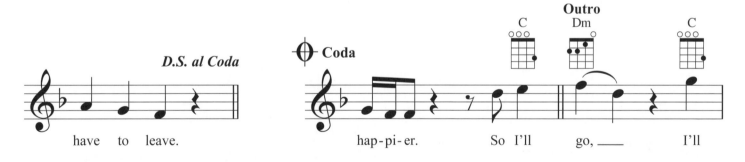

D.S. al Coda   **Coda**   **Outro**

have   to   leave.   hap - pi - er.   So I'll   go, ____   I'll

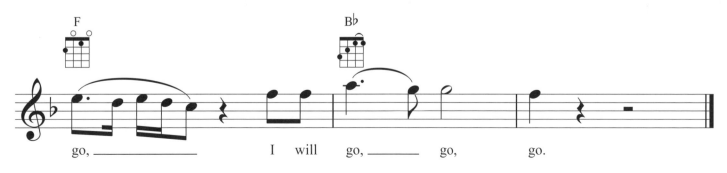

go, _____   I will   go, _____ go,   go.

Love Lies

Words and Music by Khalid Robinson, Normani Kordei Hamilton,
Tayla Parx, Jamil George Chammas and Ryan Vojtesak

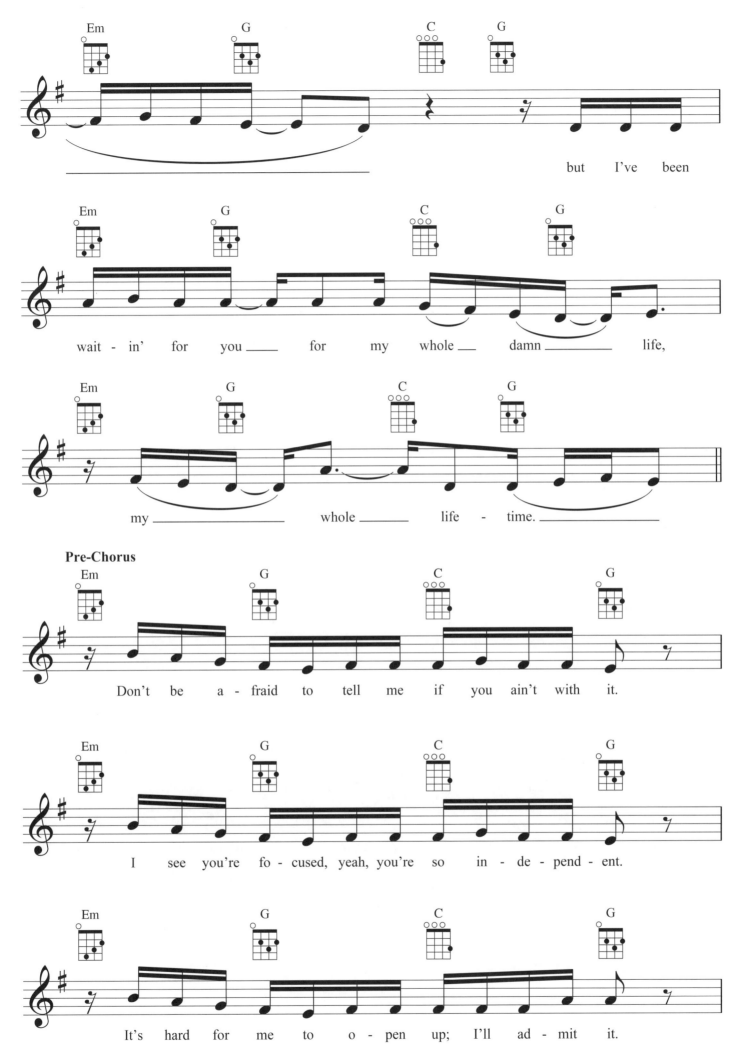

but I've been

wait - in' for you _____ for my whole ___ damn _____ life,

my _____ whole _____ life - time. _____

Pre-Chorus

Don't be a - fraid to tell me if you ain't with it.

I see you're fo - cused, yeah, you're so in - de - pend - ent.

It's hard for me to o - pen up; I'll ad - mit it.

You've got some shit to say and I'm here to lis-ten. So, ba-by,

Chorus

tell me where your love lies, ___ waste the day and spend the night. ___

Un-der-neath the sun-rise ___ show me where your love lies. ___

Verse

Female: 2. I've been so in-to your mys-ter-y.

Is it be-cause ___ of our his-to-ry?

Are you ___ in-to me? ___

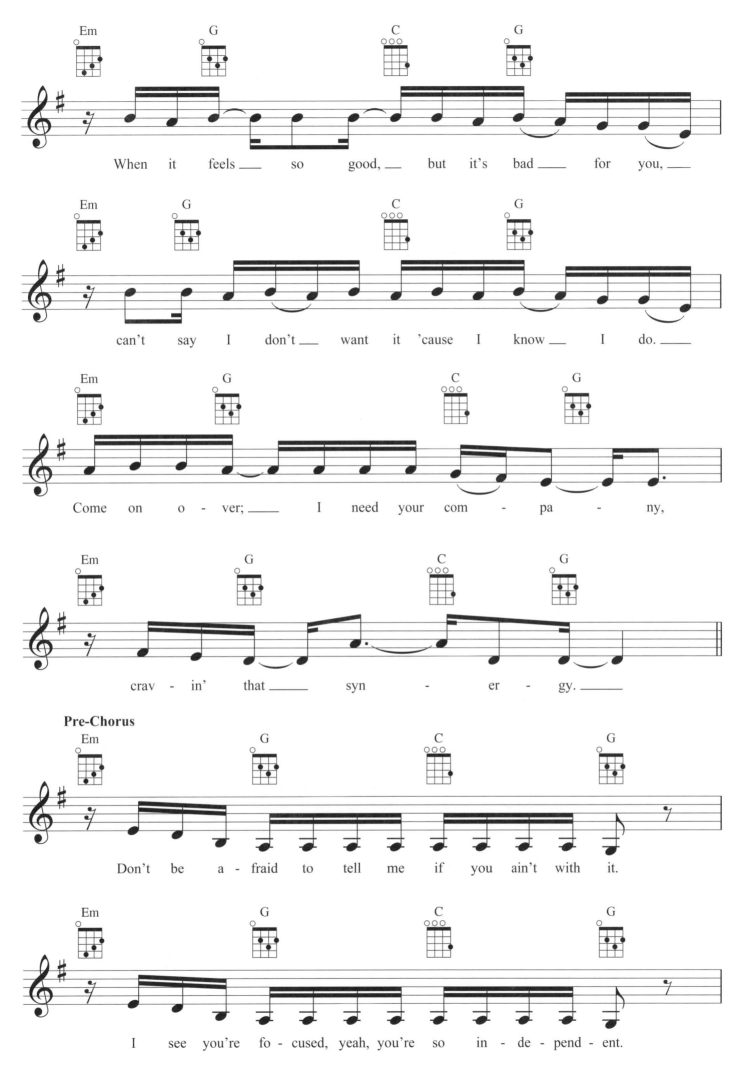

When it feels __ so good, __ but it's bad __ for you, __

can't say I don't __ want it 'cause I know __ I do. ___

Come on o-ver; __ I need your com - pa - ny,

crav - in' that ___ syn - er - gy. __

Pre-Chorus

Don't be a-fraid to tell me if you ain't with it.

I see you're fo-cused, yeah, you're so in - de - pend - ent.

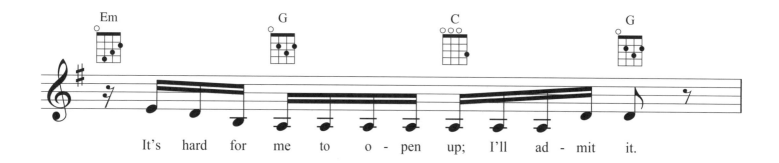

It's hard for me to o - pen up; I'll ad - mit it.

You've got some shit to say and I'm here to lis - ten. So, ba - by...

% **Chorus**

Both: Tell me where your love lies, ___ waste the day and spend the night. ___

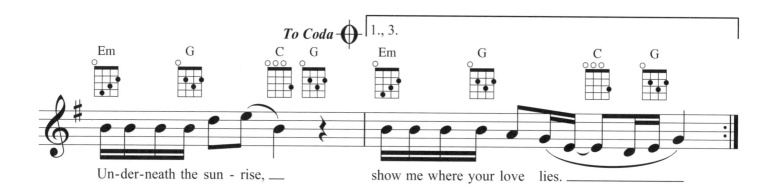

To Coda ⊕ | 1., 3.

Un-der-neath the sun - rise, ___ show me where your love lies. ___

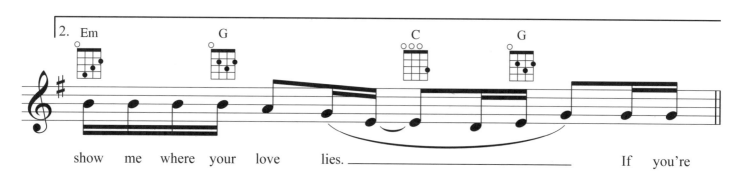

2.

show me where your love lies. _____ If you're

Bridge

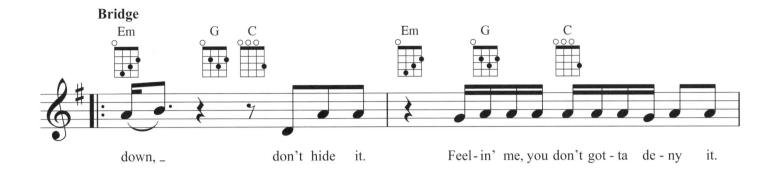

down, _ don't hide it. Feel-in' me, you don't got-ta de-ny it.

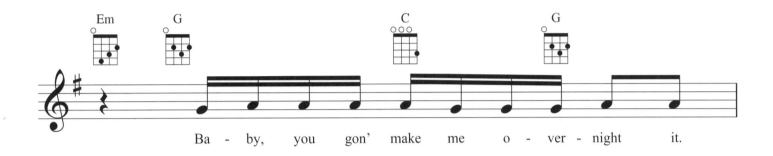

Ba - by, you gon' make me o - ver - night it.

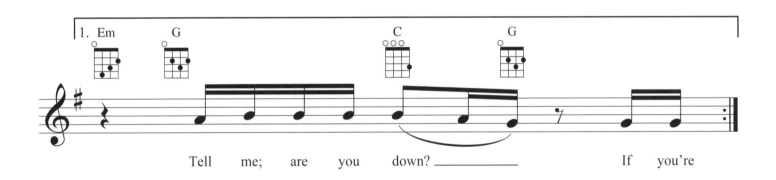

Tell me; are you down? _____ If you're

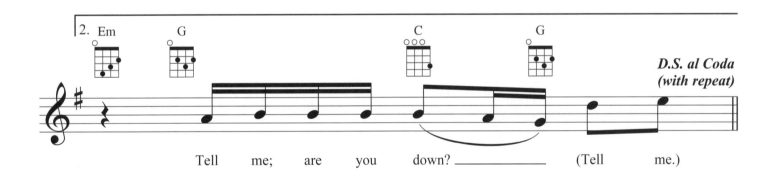

Tell me; are you down? _____ (Tell me.)

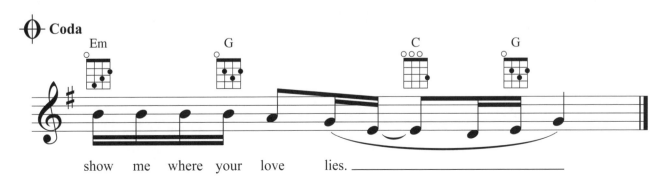

show me where your love lies. _____

Love Someone

Words and Music by Lukas Forchhammer, Morten Ristorp, Morten Pilegaard,
Jaramye Daniels, Don Stefano, David LaBrel and James Ghaleb

Verse
Moderately

1. There are days _____ I wake up and I
2. When you say _____ you love the way I

pinch my-self. You're with me, not some-one else.
make you feel, ev-'ry-thing be-comes so real.

And I'm scared, _ yeah, I'm _ still scared _ that it's
Don't be scared, _ no, don't _ be scared, _ 'cause you're

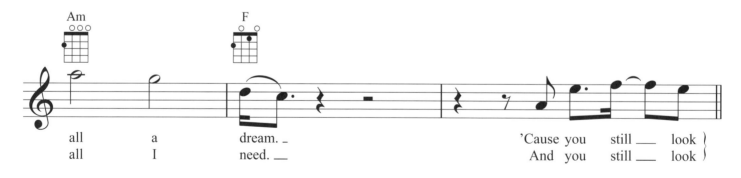

all a dream. _ 'Cause you still _ look
all I need. _ And you still _ look

Bridge

All my life, _____ I thought it'd be hard to find ___ the one till I _____ found you. ___ And I find it bit - ter - sweet _____ 'cause you gave me some - thing to lose. _____ But when you loved some - one ___ like I do. _____ You prob-'ly nev - er loved some - one _____ like I _____ do. _____

D.S. al Coda

Coda

High Hopes

**Words and Music by Brendon Urie, Samuel Hollander, William Lobban Bean,
Jonas Jeberg, Jacob Sinclair, Jenny Owen Youngs,
Ilsey Juber, Lauren Pritchard and Taylor Parks**

"Ful-fill the proph-e-cy. Be some-thing great. _ Go make a leg-a-cy."

Man-i-fest des-ti-ny. Back in the days, _ we want-ed ev-'ry-thing, want-ed

ev-'ry-thing. Ma-ma said, "Burn your bi-o-graph-ies.

Re-write your his-to-ry. Light up your wild-est dreams." Mu-se-um vic-to-ries,

ev-er-y day. _ We want-ed ev-'ry-thing, want-ed ev-'ry-thing. Ma-ma said, _

Pre-Chorus

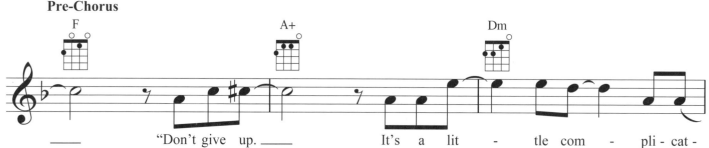

_ "Don't give up. ___ It's a lit-tle com-pli-cat-

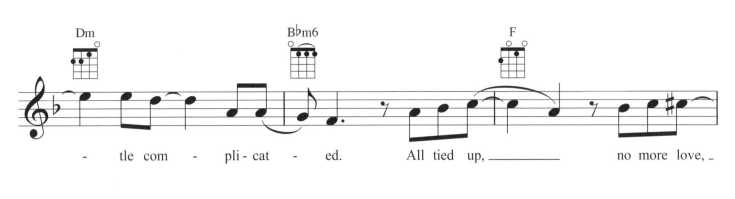

- tle com - pli - cat - ed.   All tied up, _____ no more love, _

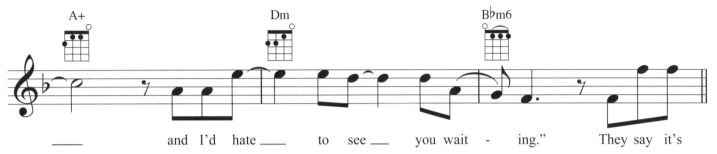

____ and I'd hate ___ to see ___ you wait - ing."   They say it's

Bridge 2

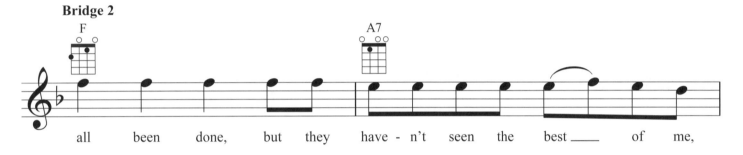

all been done, but they have - n't seen the best ___ of me,

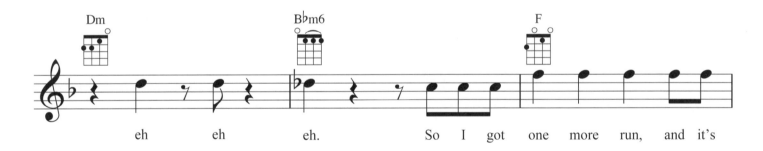

eh   eh   eh.   So I got one more run, and it's

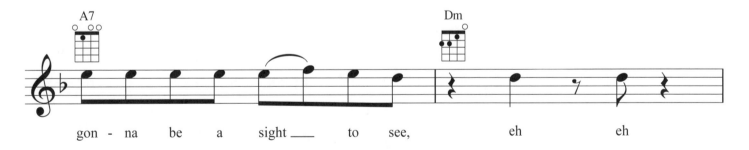

gon - na be a sight ___ to see,   eh   eh

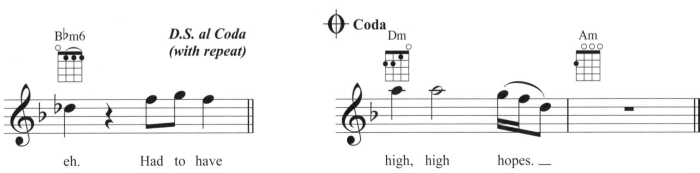

D.S. al Coda
(with repeat)

eh.   Had to have   high, high hopes. ___

Lucid Dreams

Words and Music by Jarad Higgins, Dominic Miller, Gordon Sumner, Danny Snodgrass Jr. and Nicholas Mira

make me __ feel A - O - kay. __ I know __ it's all in __ my head. I have __ these lu - cid __ dreams where I __ can't move a __ thing, __ think - ing __ of you in __ my bed. __ You were __ my ev - 'ry - thing; thoughts of __ a wed - ding __ ring. Now I'm __ just bet - ter __ off __

Bridge

__ dead. I'd do it o - ver a - gain. __ I did-n't want it to end. __

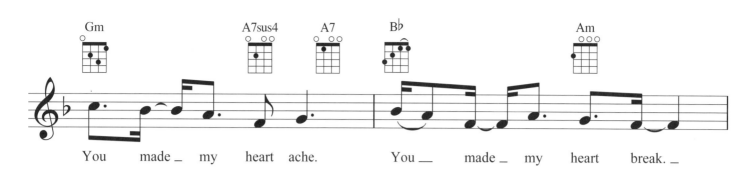

You made __ my heart ache. You __ made __ my heart break. __

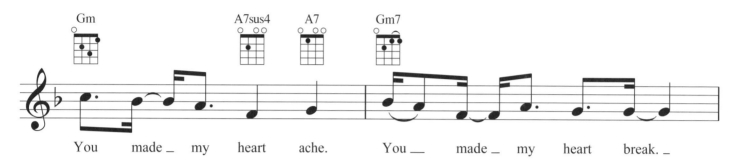

You made __ my heart ache. You __ made __ my heart break. __

D.C. al Coda (with repeat)

You made __ my heart ache. __ You __ made __ my heart break __ a - gain. _____

_____ the one. Lis - ten - ing to my heart in - stead of my head. _

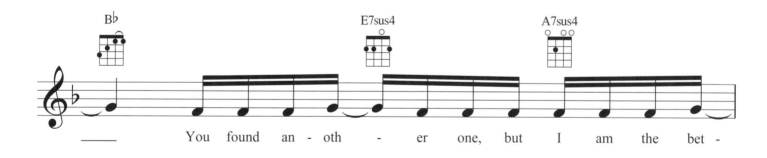

_____ You found an - oth - er one, but I am the bet -

- ter one. I won't let you for - get me.

Natural

Words and Music by Dan Reynolds, Wayne Sermon, Ben McKee, Daniel Platzman,
Justin Trantor, Mattias Larsson and Robin Fredricksson

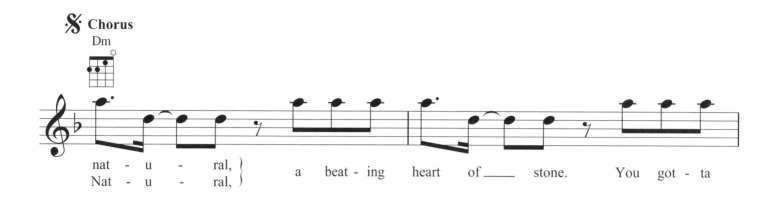

nat - u - ral, } Nat - u - ral, } a beat - ing heart of ___ stone. You got - ta

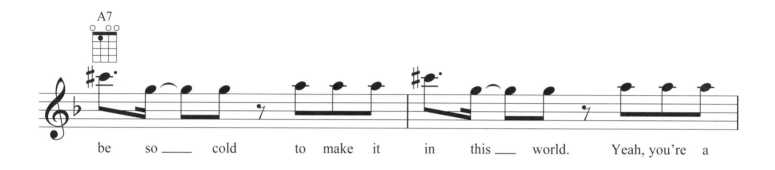

be so ___ cold to make it in this ___ world. Yeah, you're a

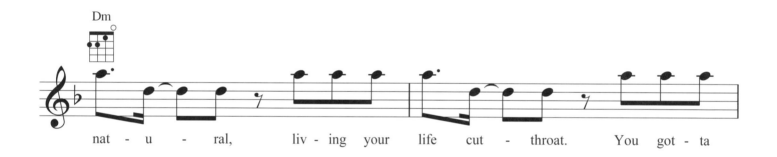

nat - u - ral, liv - ing your life cut - throat. You got - ta

To Coda ⊕ **Bridge**

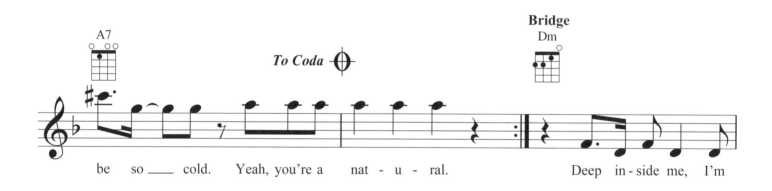

be so ___ cold. Yeah, you're a nat - u - ral. Deep in - side me, I'm

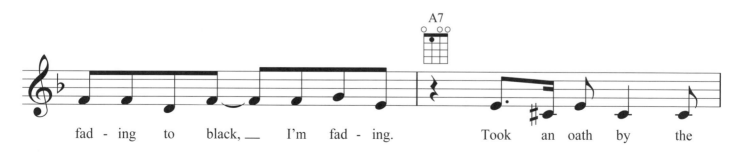

fad - ing to black, ___ I'm fad - ing. Took an oath by the

blood of my hand, ___ won't break it. I can taste it; the

end is up - on ___ us, I swear. Gon - na make it,

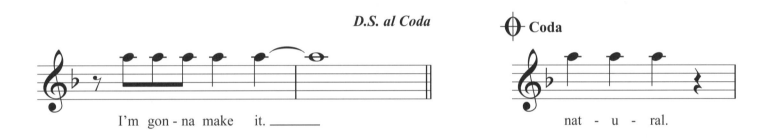

D.S. al Coda

⊕ **Coda**

I'm gon - na make it. _____

nat - u - ral.

Outro

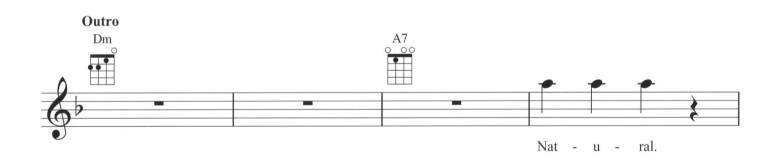

Nat - u - ral.

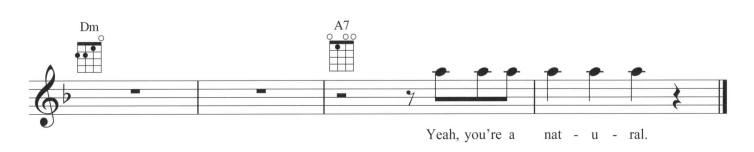

Yeah, you're a nat - u - ral.

Shallow

from A STAR IS BORN

Words and Music by Stefani Germanotta, Mark Ronson, Andrew Wyatt and Anthony Rossomando

* Male vocal written at sung pitch.

Chorus

I'm off the deep ____ end. Watch as I dive ____ in:

I'll nev - er meet ___ the ground. _____ Crash through the sur - face,

where they can't hurt ___ us. We're far from the shal - low now. ____

Both: In the shal, -al, shal - low, __ in the shal, __ shal, -al,

-al, -al - low. ___ In the shal, -al, shal - low, __ we're

far from the shal - low now. ____

Sunflower

from SPIDER-MAN: INTO THE SPIDER-VERSE
Words and Music by Austin Richard Post, Louis Bell, Swae Lee,
Billy Walsh, Carl Rosen, Carter Lang and Khalif Brown

First note

Verse
Moderately

1. Need-less to say, I keep her in check. She was all bad - bad, nev-er-the - less.

Call-ing it quits now, ba - by, I'm a wreck. Crash at my place, ba - by, you're a wreck.

Need-less to say, I'm keep-ing her in check. She was a bad - bad, nev - er - the - less.

Call-ing it quits now, ba - by, I'm a wreck. Crash at my place, ba - by, you're a wreck.

Think-ing in a bad way, los-ing your grip. Scream-ing at my face, ba - by, don't trip.

Some-one took a big L, don't know how that felt. _ Look-ing at you side-ways, par-ty on tilt.

Pre-Chorus

Ooh, _____ some things you just can't re - fuse. _____ She wan-na

ride like a cruise, _____ and I'm not tryin' to lose. _____

Chorus

Then you're left in the dust un - less I stuck by ya.

You're the sun - flow - er. I think your love would be too much,

or you'll be left in the dust un - less I stuck by ya. You're the sun - flow - er,

Verse

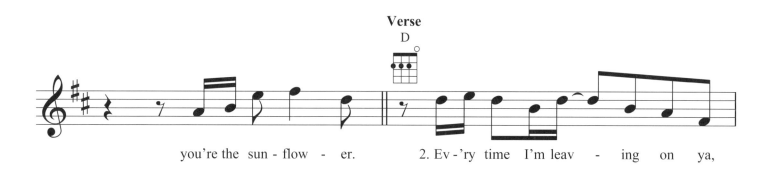

you're the sun - flow - er.　　2. Ev - 'ry time I'm leav - ing on ya,

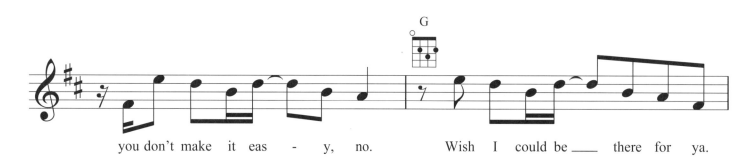

you don't make it eas - y, no.　　Wish I could be ___ there for ya.

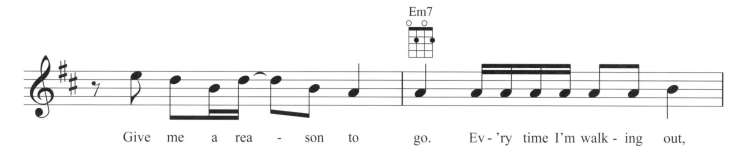

Give me a rea - son to go.　　Ev - 'ry time I'm walk - ing out,

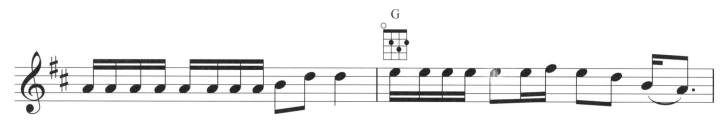

I can hear you tell - ing me to turn a - round.　　Fight-ing for my trust, say you won't back down, _

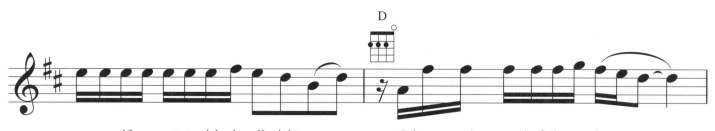

e - ven if we got-ta risk it all right now. _　　I know you're scared of the un - known, _____

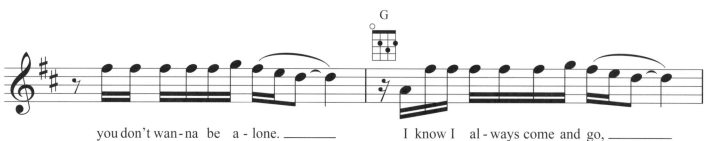

you don't wan-na be a - lone. _____　　I know I al - ways come and go, _____

Outro-Chorus

but it's out of my con-trol. _____ Then you'll be left in the dust

un-less I stuck by ya. You're the sun-flow-er.

I think your love would be too much, or you'll be left in the dust

un-less I stuck by ya. You're the sun-flow-er,

you're the sun-flow-er.

Thank U, Next

Words and Music by Ariana Grande, Victoria McCants, Kimberly Krysiuk,
Taylor Parks, Tommy Brown, Charles Anderson and Michael Foster

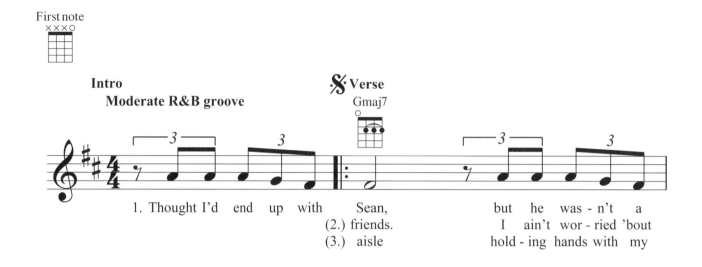

thank - ful.   Wish I could say "thank you" to   Mal - colm, _   'cause he was an
last, ___   'cause her name is   Ar - i, ____   and I'm so good with
last. ___   God for - bid some-thing hap - pens. _   'Least this song is   a

Pre-Chorus

an - gel. __   One taught _ me love,   one taught _ me
that. _____   She taught _ me love,   she taught _ me
smash. _____   I've got so ___ much love,   got so ___ much

pa - tience, _ and one taught _ me pain.   Now I'm so ___ a -
pa - tience. _ How she han - dles pain,   that shit's _ a -
pa - tience. _ I've learned from __ the pain.   It turned out ___ a -

mazed as ___ I've loved and __ I've lost.   But that's not __ what
maz - ing. __ I've loved and __ I've lost,   but that's not __ what
maz - ing. __ I've loved and __ I've lost,   but that's not __ what

I see, __ so look what __ I got.   Look what __ you
I see, __ 'cause look what __ I found.   No need __ for
I see, __ 'cause look what __ I found.   No need __ for

taught me. __
search - ing. __
search - ing. __
And __ for __ that __ I ____ say: Thank u, ____ next,

next. Thank u, ____ next, next. Thank u, ____ next. I'm so fuck-ing grate-ful for my

ex. Thank u, ____ next, next. Thank u, ____ next, next. Thank u, ____ next.

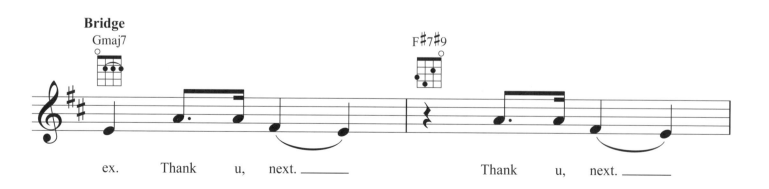

I'm so fuck - ing... 2. Spend more time with my   I'm so fuck-ing grate-ful for my

ex. Thank u, next. ____   Thank u, next. ____

Thank u, next. _____ I'm so fuck-ing... 3. One day I'll walk down that

Bridge

I'm so fuck-ing grate-ful for my ex. Thank u, next. _____

Thank u, next. ___ Thank u, next. _____ Yeah, ee.

Thank u, next. ___ Thank u, next. ___ Thank u, next. _____

Outro

Repeat and fade

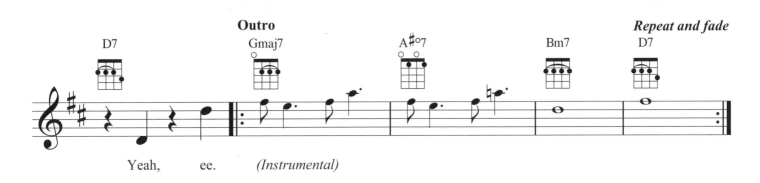

Yeah, ee. *(Instrumental)*

Without Me

Words and Music by Ashley Frangipane, Brittany Amaradio, Carl Rosen, Justin Timberlake, Scott Storch, Louis Bell, Amy Allen and Timothy Mosley

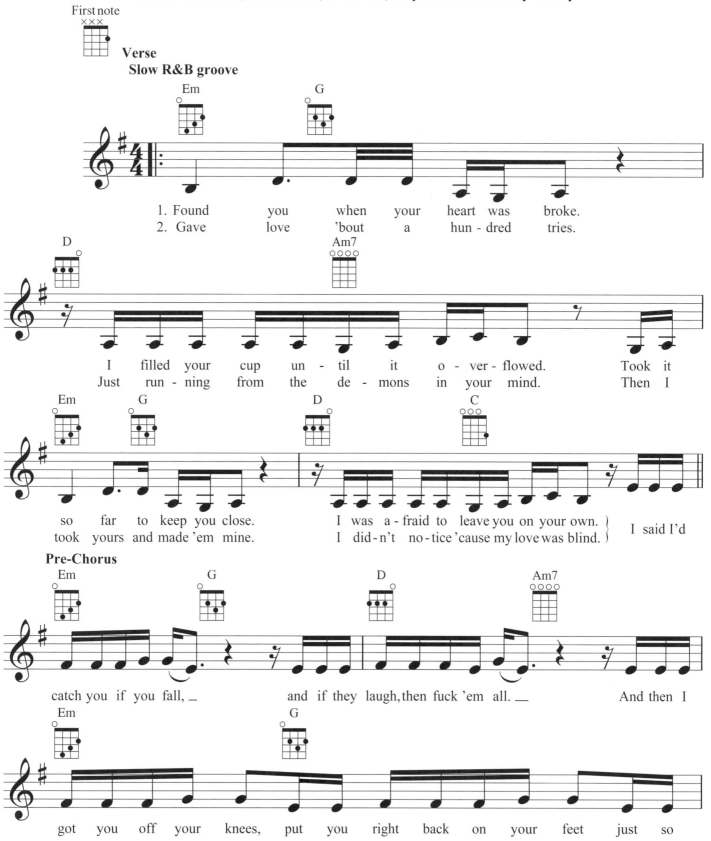

1. Found you when your heart was broke.
2. Gave love 'bout a hun-dred tries.

I filled your cup un-til it o-ver-flowed. Took it
Just run-ning from the de-mons in your mind. Then I

so far to keep you close. I was a-fraid to leave you on your own.
took yours and made 'em mine. I did-n't no-tice 'cause my love was blind.
I said I'd

Pre-Chorus

catch you if you fall, _ and if they laugh, then fuck 'em all. _ And then I

got you off your knees, put you right back on your feet just so

you could take ad-van-tage of me. ____ Tell me: how's it

% **Chorus**

feel ___ sit-ting up there, feel-ing so high, but too far a-way to hold me? You know I'm the

one who put you up there, name in the sky; does it ev-er get lone-ly think-ing you could

live _____ with-out ____ me, ____ think-ing you could

live _____ with-out ____ me? Ba-by, I'm the

To Coda ⊕

one who put you up there. I don't know why.(Yeah, I don't know why.) Think-ing you could

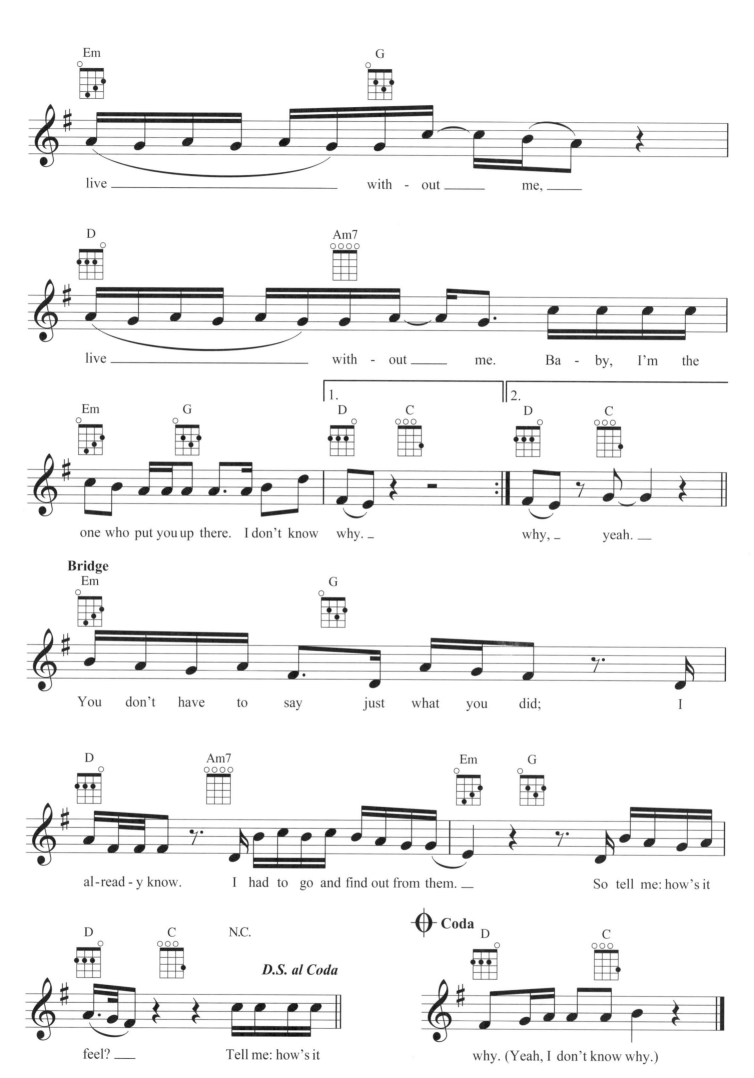

Nothing Breaks Like a Heart

**Words and Music by Mark Ronson, Miley Cyrus, Thomas Brenneck,
Conor Szymanski, Ilsey Juber, Maxime Picard and Clement Picard**

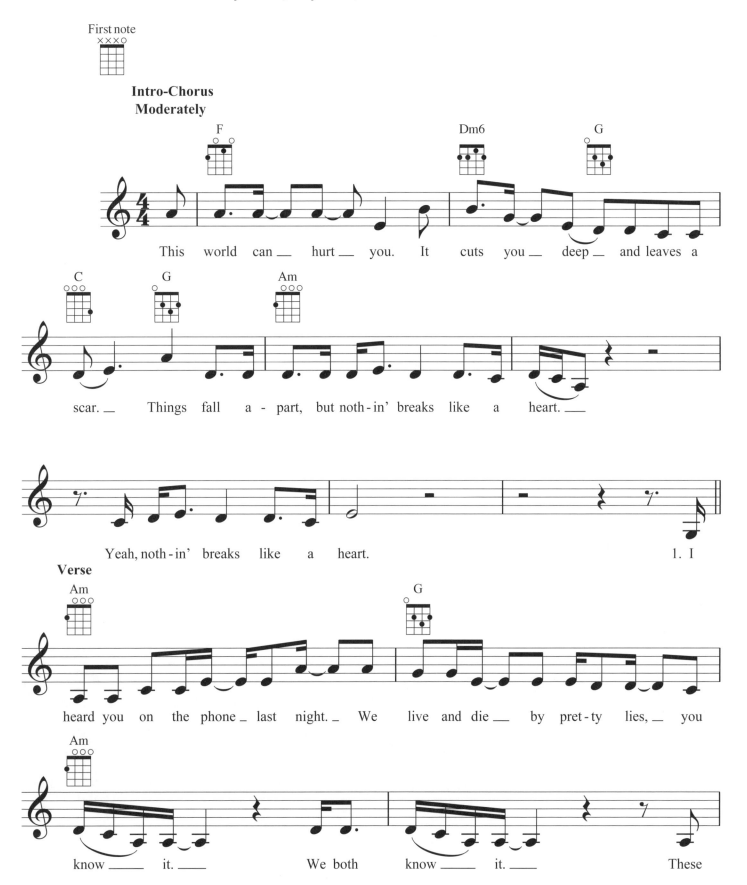

sil - ver bul - let cig - a - rettes, _ this burn - in' house, _ there's noth -in' left. _ It's

smok - in', _ we both know _ it. _ We

got all night to fall _ in love, _ but just like that we fall a - part. _ We're

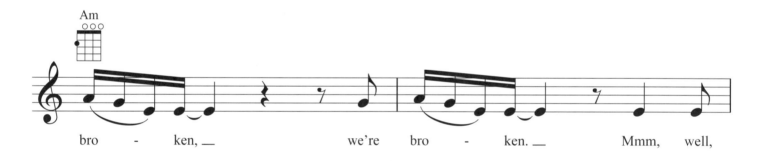

bro - ken, _ we're bro - ken. _ Mmm, well,

noth - in', noth - in', noth - in' _ gon' save us _ now. Well, there's

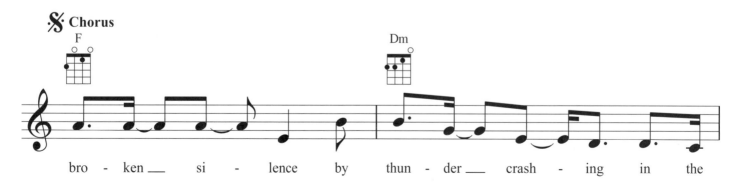

𝄋 **Chorus**

bro - ken _ si - lence by thun - der _ crash - ing in the

dark. (Crash in the dark.) And this bro-ken ___ rec-ord spin

end-less ___ cir-cles in the bar. (Spin 'round in the bar.) This

world can ___ hurt ___ you. It cuts you ___ deep ___ and leaves a

scar. Things fall a-part, but noth-in' breaks like a heart. ___ Mmm, ___

To Coda 1
To Coda 2

___ noth-in' breaks like a heart. 2. We'll

Verse

leave each oth-er cold as ice ___ and high and dry. ___ The des-ert wind ___ is

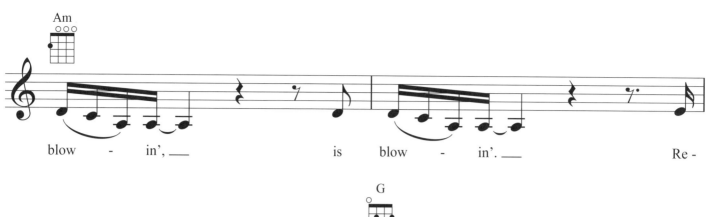

blow - in', ___ is blow - in'. ___ Re -

mem - ber what you said to me? __ We were drunk in love __ in Ten - nes - see __ and I

hold ___ it, ___ we both know ___ it. ___ Mmm, there's

noth - in', noth - in', noth - in' ___ gon' save us now.

D.S. al Coda 1

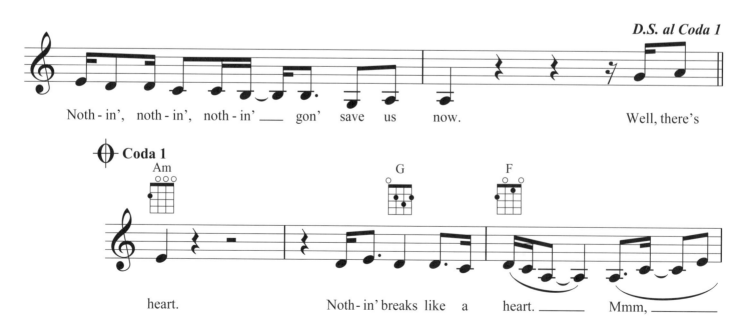

Noth - in', noth - in', noth - in' ___ gon' save us now. Well, there's

⊕ **Coda 1**

heart. Noth - in' breaks like a heart. ___ Mmm, ___

noth-in' breaks like a heart.

Pre-Chorus

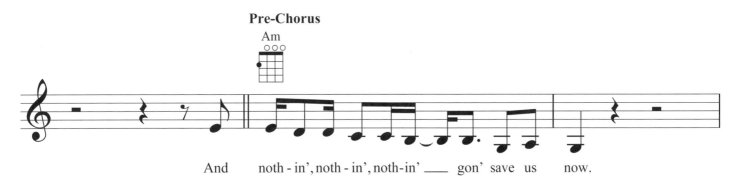

And noth-in', noth-in', noth-in' ___ gon' save us now.

D.S. al Coda 2

Noth-in', noth-in', noth-in' ___ gon' save us now. Mmm, there's

Coda 2

Am   G

heart.   Noth-in' breaks like a

Outro

F   Dm

heart. ___   Mmm, ___   noth-in' breaks like a

Am

heart.

Youngblood

**Words and Music by Ashton Irwin, Calum Hood, Louis Bell,
Luke Hemming, Alexandra Tamposi and Andrew Watt**

First note

Verse
Moderately fast

1. Re-mem - ber the words you told me: __ love __ me 'til the day I

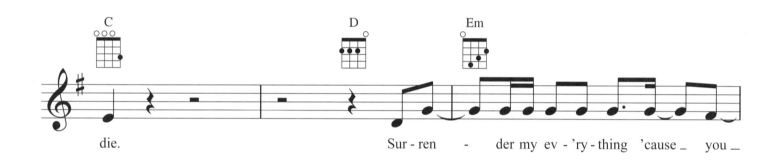

die. Sur - ren - der my ev - 'ry-thing 'cause __ you __

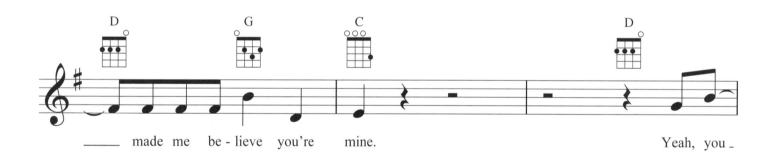

__ made me be - lieve you're mine. Yeah, you __

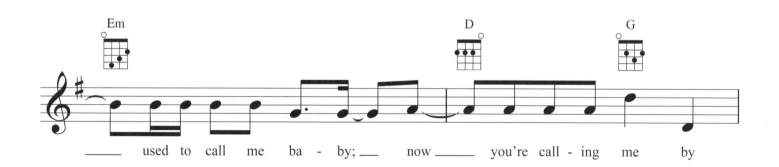

__ used to call me ba - by; __ now __ you're call - ing me by

name.   (Mm.)   Takes — one to know one, yeah, you — beat —

— me   at   my   own   damn   game.   You

Pre-Chorus

push and you push and I'm pull-ing a-way,   pull-ing a-way   from   you.   I

give and I give and I give and you take,   give and you take.   Young-

Chorus

blood,   say you want me,   say you   want   me   out   of your life, —

____   and I'm   just   a   dead   man   walk-ing to-night. —

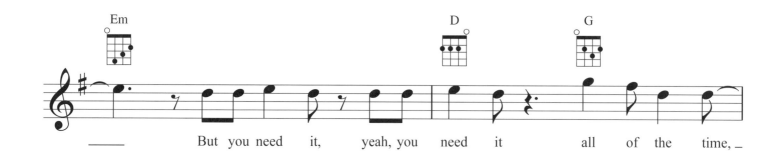

But you need it, yeah, you need it all of the time, __

__ yeah. (Ooh, __ ooh, __ ooh.) __ Young -

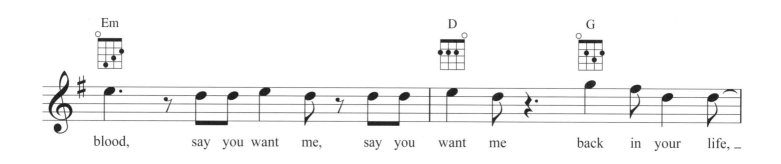

blood, say you want me, say you want me back in your life, __

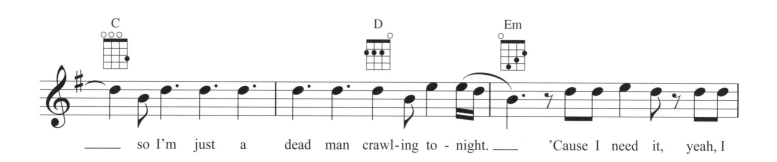

__ so I'm just a dead man crawl-ing to-night. __ 'Cause I need it, yeah, I

To Coda 1

To Coda 2

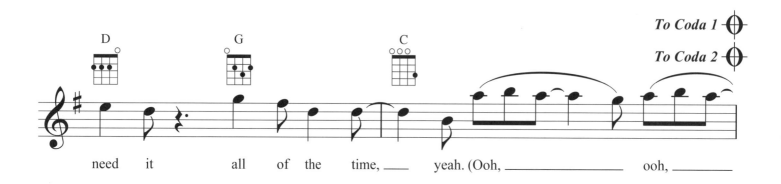

need it all of the time, __ yeah. (Ooh, __ ooh, __

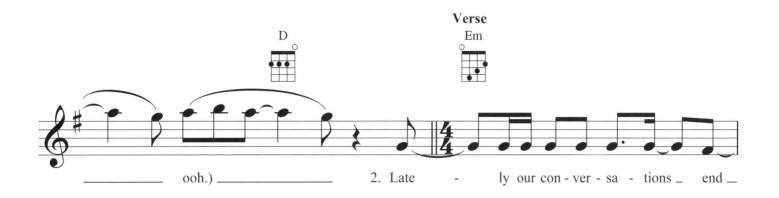

Verse

_____ ooh.) _____ 2. Late - ly our con - ver - sa - tions _ end _

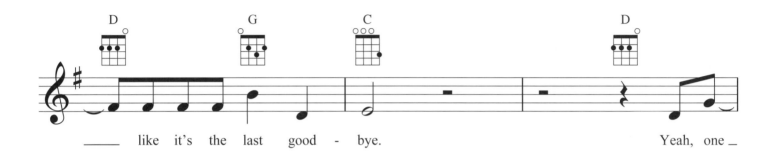

_____ like it's the last good - bye. Yeah, one _

_____ of us gets too drunk and _ calls _____ a - bout a hun - dred

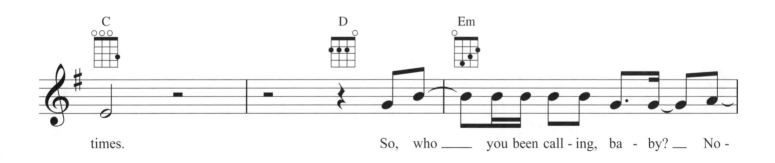

times. So, who _____ you been call - ing, ba - by? _ No -

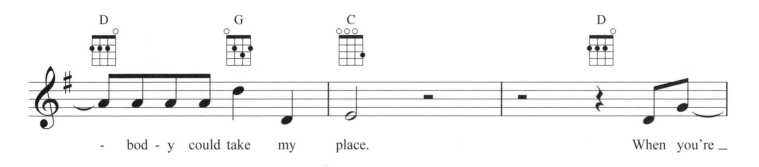

- bod - y could take my place. When you're _

_____ look-ing at those stran - gers, _ hope _____ to God you see my face.

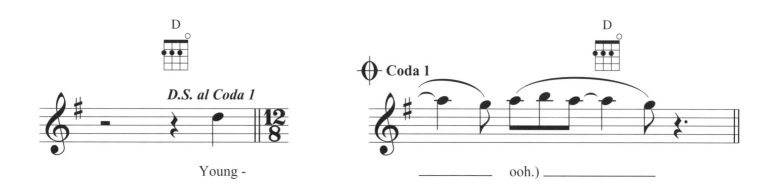

D.S. al Coda 1

Young -

Coda 1

_____ ooh.) _____

Bridge

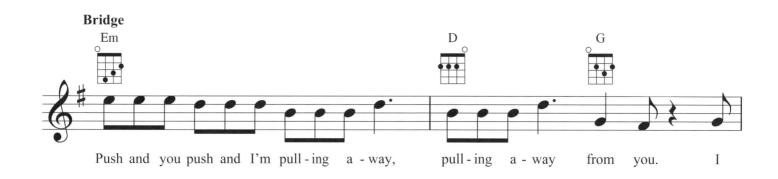

Push and you push and I'm pull-ing a - way, pull-ing a - way from you. I

give and I give and I give and you take, give and you take. I'm

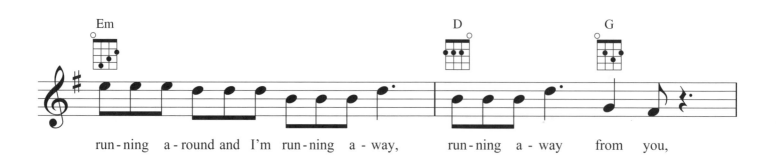

run-ning a - round and I'm run-ning a - way, run-ning a - way from you,

mm, from you. Young -

Outro

_____ ooh.) _____ You push and you push and I'm pull-ing a-way,

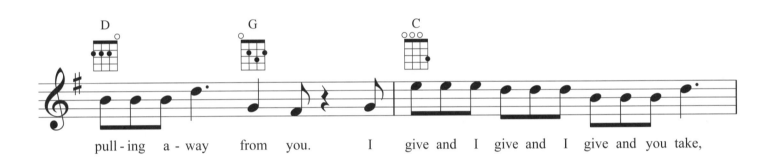

pull-ing a-way from you. I give and I give and I give and you take,

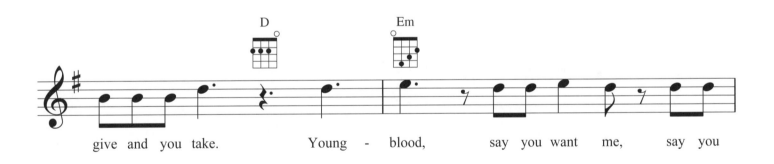

give and you take. Young - blood, say you want me, say you

want me out of your life ____ and I'm just a dead man walk-ing to - night.

You Say

Words and Music by Lauren Daigle, Jason Ingram and Paul Mabury

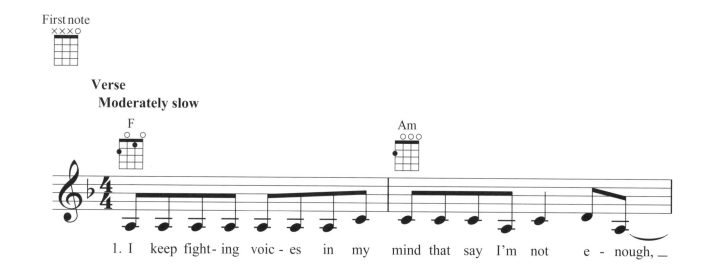

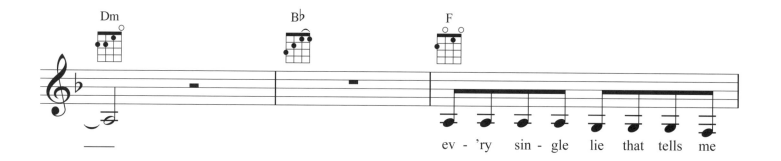

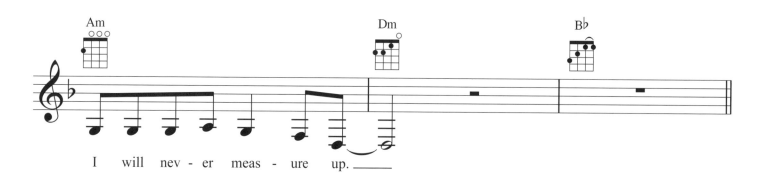

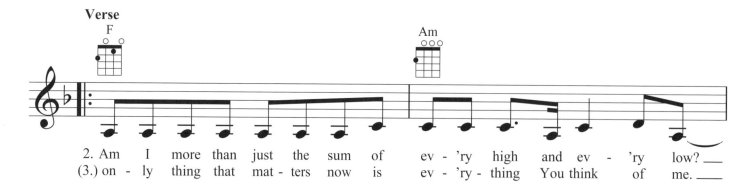